D0729298

Public Talk Series: 3

NEED FOR COGNITIVE CHANGE

Swami Dayananda Saraswati
Arsha Vidya

Arsha Vidya
Research and Publication Trust
Chennai

Published by :
Arsha Vidya Research
and Publication Trust
32 / 4 ' Sri Nidhi ' Apts III Floor
Sir Desika Road Mylapore
Chennai 600 004 INDIA
Tel : 044 2499 7023
Telefax : 2499 7131
Email : avrandpc@gmail.com

ISBN : 978 - 93 - 80049 - 01 - 4

First Edition : June 2006 Copies : 1000
1st Reprint : May 2009 Copies : 2000

Design :
Suchi Ebrahim

Printed by :
Sudarsan Graphics
27, Neelakanta Mehta Street
T. Nagar, Chennai 600 017
Email : info@sudarsan.com

Contents

PREFACE

I am very happy to see in print the series of talks I gave in Chennai under different titles for meaningful 'Living'. I enjoyed my reading these manuscripts inasmuch as the material therein was an outcome of my open thinking. In fact in some places I was amused as well as surprised. Anyone who reads this book, I am sure, will find it refreshingly useful. I congratulate the dedicated people at the Arsha Vidya Research and Publication Trust, for this thoughtful publication.

Swami Dayananda Saraswati

Rishikesh
27 May 2006

Key to Transliteration and Pronunciation of Sanskrit Letters

Sanskrit is a highly phonetic language and hence accuracy in articulation of the letters is important. For those unfamiliar with the *Devanägari* script, the international transliteration is a guide to the proper pronunciation of Sanskrit letters.

अ	*a*	*(but)*
आ	*ā*	*(father)*
इ	*i*	*(it)*
ई	*ī*	*(beat)*
उ	*u*	*(full)*
ऊ	*ū*	*(pool)*
ऋ	*ṛ*	*(rhythm)*
ॠ	*ṝ*	*(marine)*
ऌ	*ḷ*	*(revelry)*
ए	*e*	*(play)*
ऐ	*ai*	*(aisle)*
ओ	*o*	*(go)*
औ	*au*	*(loud)*
क	*ka*	*(seek)* 1
ख	*kha*	*(blockhead)**1
ग	*ga*	*(get)* 1
घ	*gha*	*(log hut)**1
ङ	*ṅa*	*(sing)* 1
च	*ca*	*(chunk)* 2
छ	*cha*	*(catch him)**2
ज	*ja*	*(jump)* 2
झ	*jha*	*(hedgehog)**2
ञ	*ña*	*(bunch)* 2
ट	*öa*	*(true)**3
ठ	*öha*	*(anthill)**3
ड	*òa*	*(drum)**3
ढ	*òha*	*(godhead)**3
ण	*ëa*	*(under)**3
त	*ta*	*(path)**4
थ	*tha*	*(thunder)**4
द	*da*	*(that)**4
ध	*dha*	*(breathe)**4
न	*na*	*(nut)**4
प	*pa*	*(put)* 5
फ	*pha*	*(loophole)**5
ब	*ba*	*(bin)* 5
भ	*bha*	*(abhor)**5
म	*ma*	*(much)* 5
य	*ya*	*(loyal)*
र	*ra*	*(red)*
ल	*la*	*(luck)*
व	*va*	*(vase)*
श	*ça*	*(sure)*
ष	*ña*	*(shun)*
स	*sa*	*(so)*
ह	*ha*	*(hum)*

•	à	*anusvära*	(nasalisation of preceding vowel)
:	ù	*visarga*	(aspiration of preceding vowel)
*			No exact English equivalents for these letters

1.	Guttural	–	Pronounced from throat
2.	Palatal	–	Pronounced from palate
3.	Lingual	–	Pronounced from cerebrum
4.	Dental	–	Pronounced from teeth
5.	Labial	–	Pronounced from lips

The 5th letter of each of the above class – called nasals – are also pronounced nasally.

TALK 1

INTRODUCTION

There is always a need for change. In every generation and even in the Stone Age, there were people who felt a great need for change—change in terms of environment, people's well-being, political situation, infrastructure for economic growth and so on. I think the need for change was always there. However, need for cognitive change is a little different. The vision that I should change the society or a given situation for my well-being or for others' has to undergo a change. A scientist once remarked, "If I have a hammer in my hand, I see everything around me as nails alone."

If we look at the way we have gathered this large body of knowledge that is modern science, it reveals something very significant to us. The general thinking is, progress has always been linear, a step-by-step movement. Be it physics, nuclear physics or any discipline, the common perception is, science has reached this point by progressing linearly. It is not true. There is certain body of knowledge at a given time, in a given discipline in the human history. Further, this knowledge has been gathered within certain structure. The structure implies a set of assumptions called paradigms. It is within the paradigms alone that research is advanced. These paradigms appear to be fixed and form the basic framework. Any clarity or change that we are able to glean, lies within and not outside this framework.

Therefore, it implies that we cannot know anything more than we already know, since we cannot change the paradigms. However, this is not true. We have been changing. We have been dropping old assumptions, indicating that progress in science is not linear. It is always frog leaping. It leaps from one stage to another. In the process, more often than not, old assumptions are dropped, and in their place new assumptions crop up. Later these form the new framework which again are replaced. There is a miracle happening. Every time we discover something, and when the discovery does not rest within the known framework, the paradigms shift.

Classical physics looked at the physical universe in a certain way. Time was absolute; space was absolute. These concepts and assumptions had to be dropped when they were found to be as relative as anything else. Therefore, in changes such as these, you always see the miracle of knowledge taking place. You do not see what you do not know, and unless you know, you do not see. Again, unless you see, you cannot know further. It is a catch-22 situation. Yet you find that you do come to learn, to know. You can see this miracle of knowledge. However, it is not a miracle for a person who understands Vedanta. Our ancestors have observed this. In every generation, they observed and learned that knowledge is something that happens, and it often happens in quantum leaps.

If you observe what is going on in every field, there is an urgent feeling that something needs to be done. To cite an example, countries in Europe came together and created a euro dollar. Perhaps later, there will be an American dollar for both North and South America. Maybe there will be an Asian dollar. Still later, there may be one global dollar. Even in our monetary system, the need for change is felt. The political systems have changed. Once upon a time they thought that communism would solve all the problems, not knowing it also causes many problems. Later it was thought that democracy would solve the problems. It was also thought that without monarchy every problem could be solved. Thus, the world over, people felt the need for change.

I always hear that people should change in terms of their character, their value systems. In this area, a lot of change has already taken place. In the west, for instance, I find there is a movement of support groups such as those for recovering addicts, for people who want to cut down obesity, for the physically challenged and many more. It is a big movement and shows that there is certain change. People have come to recognise the need to change.

Talk 2

AREAS REQUIRING COGNITIVE CHANGE

Notwithstanding all these changes, a human being has to face himself or herself as a person. It is a problem. If the elephants find that there is no water in the area that they live in, they migrate. In winter if the birds in Siberia find it very cold, they migrate to places where there is sun and water. It is the extent of their need for change. They need to change only the place or situation. They do not need a cognitive change to change themselves because they do not have complexes that we have. A human being may have evolved from a monkey but he has complexes that the monkey fortunately does not have. These complexes were always there. It is not that only modern man has complexes. Our forefathers also had, but I think they could manage their complexes better than us, if the human restlessness is any indication.

Restlessness in human pursuits

I have been thinking on these lines for some time. What is the reason for the extra restlessness that we see in human pursuits? For instance, modern music is an expression of this restlessness. The singer cannot sit still and sing; he has to dance to the music. The one who listens to the music also cannot sit still; he or she has to 'do' music. As for the lyrics, they do not have any content. If you take modern art, it looks to me as though it does not require much time or effort to produce many pieces a day. I may be wrong totally; I would like to be wrong. All of this indicates an inner restlessness.

Competition in childhood - the reason for human restlessness

Inner restlessness must have some specific cause. The cause is very obvious to me. It is something that I picked up from the *upaniṣad*s. Śvetaketu, the son of Uddālaka, was twelve years old when his father sent him to a *gurukula*. He spent twelve years at the *gurukula* and returned home when he was twenty four. It means the child was with its parents for twelve full years. Perhaps in the *gurukula* there were no examinations. Even if the child is made to compete after it is twelve years old, I do not think there would be a serious problem.

I find that the modern mental illnesses are due to competition we impose on the child when it is barely three or four years old. Please note that it is not the examinations; it is the child that is asked to compete. When the child is in a formative stage, competition will definitely damage its self-opinion. One cannot compete without picking up the sense that he or she is a failure, is no good, or not that good. Even the one who succeeds has to maintain that particular status; pressure is inevitable. It is important for a child to win the approval of its parents. So it wants to compete and be the best. This puts pressure on the child which is further compounded by parental pressure. No child is exempt from this pressure, not even the one who performs well.

The child has problems of proving himself or herself at an age when it has to play and relax at home. It is obvious that from the first year onwards, no child is going to score the maximum in all subjects, every time. Even in terms of games, sports events, there are complexes all of which create problems. Every child has a feeling that he or she did not do well. There is no child who does not want to do well in sports and in the various academic subjects.

The sense of competition is not just for one year. It starts from Kindergarten and even before, at the pre KG level. I would not be surprised if it starts at the pre natal level itself. In fact, we register the child's name for school even before it is born. How shameless we have become. I think this is where a cognitive change is required. The whole society, humanity, has to undergo a thorough change in its way of looking at success, in its way of looking at what makes a person mature. Humanity is ignorant. We are pushing our children who are not to be pushed. Therefore, we have a society, a crop of people, who have complexes, nothing but complexes.

Our forefathers were better off even without Vedanta

Consequently, we can no longer be like our forefathers. They performed their daily rituals, *nitya-karma*. Most of them did not study Vedanta, *Gītā* and other *śāstra*s. Even if they did study *śāstra*, it was certainly not Vedanta. Vedanta was always meant only for the objective, mature people, *adhikārin*s. It was never taught to the general public. The students used to search for a teacher and would approach him with all propriety. The teacher would test whether[1] the student was eligible, only then admit him in the *gurukula*. In the *upaniṣad*s it is said that even Indra, the chief of the Gods, was asked to stay at the *gurukula* for thirty years, tending the cattle and performing other domestic chores, before he was taught. This was the structure of society. Vedanta was taught only to the chosen, that too only when asked; it was never given away. Perhaps it was not necessary either.

People were happy even without Vedanta. They had the leisure to listen to music and music itself was leisurely. As for literature, the volumes of poetry, *purāṇa*s and *itihāsa*s, attest to the leisure they had, to compose, study and listen to those verses. They lived a leisurely life, a life of inner leisure, although externally, without machines and technology, they had to do most of the work themselves.

Today, we have all the modern conveniences to get through our daily chores, but we do not have the inner leisure our forefathers had. Their leisure was because of the absence of competition when they were children. There is no other reason. The absence of competition is the only reason that our forefathers were more or less sane. They were content with whatever they had. As a child, I had seen in the village, women preparing and making *dosas*.[2]

---

[1] Whether or not is a common expression but the correct usage is only 'whether' without being followed by 'or not'. Whether one likes this, grammatically this is right (Author).

[2] A popular South Indian delicacy, rice pancake that comes in many varieties, flavours. Ideally a breakfast item, it is also eaten as a snack all through the day.

Every evening they would prepare the batter and make the *dosas* in the morning, a lifetime spent on domestic chores. We think that they have wasted their time. However, when I recall, I find that they were definitely happy. They used to sing while doing their work. They even had special songs for making *appalams*.[3] I have seen women transplanting rice saplings in the fields with songs in their lips. They were definitely happy. It looks to me they were contented.

Coming back to competition, I do not say examinations are bad, nor is the school system bad; I do not make any judgement. All I say is a child should not be made to compete when it is not emotionally ready to compete. A child has to be a child. It is the apple of its parents' eyes, their darling. A child has to be fondled and made to feel that he or she has brought the fullness of joy to the home. Even Kālidāsa, who had no children of his own, said that it is such a joy for a man when his child, covered with dust, runs and hugs him, calling him, 'Dad,' even though the father has just had his bath.

Need for change within

Our society now has become very complex. We need to change. We have changed the environment sufficiently; we have to continuously change it, perhaps. All these changes notwithstanding, we have to face ourselves as human beings and we have to undergo certain changes. We are not interested in changing the system. Let us know what

[3] A kind of wafer made of black gram flour, eaten either fried or roasted.

we can do now, so that we have the same leisure that our forefathers had.

You need to learn, to see that the problems you have are due to your own background. You have to see how much is self-creation and how much is not. There are many notions floating around some of which you subscribe to. There are notions propagated by religious people. There are notions caused by people who are supposed to know these things and advise you. So you have problems created by others and by yourself.

When you become a problem to yourself, there is very little left with you to deal with the problems you face every day. You have neither the time nor the inner space even to know that there is a problem. I do not say, at this point, how much is God-creation and how much is self-creation. But you definitely need to know how much is self-creation and how much is not. It needs a change in your cognition about you, about things that you want to accomplish in your life, things that are legitimately sought after. You need to undergo a change.

Knowledge of external world does not help to face myself

The universe is very vast no doubt. I know that it is an expanding universe with galaxies constantly moving away. It is impossible for the human mind to fathom the contents of the universe. If I look at myself in relation to the vastness of the universe, I do not need anyone else to give me a complex. I am inconsequential, insignificant, not even a speck in the vast universe. Nevertheless, even this vast universe has to enter, has to be known by me, within the few inches between my ears, within my mind. It is definitely a saving grace. Whatever happens or exists within these few inches of my head is what I see out there in the world.

If I have a *mālā*, garland, in my hand and you see it as a *mālā*, there is no problem. If, however, there is an old *mālā* lying around, but what you see is a huge snake, then you have to deal with the problem of a snake that does not exist, and has nothing to do with the reality of the external world. Understand this very well. You never see what is there. You always see what you think is there. You see only to the extent you know. You do not see what you do not know.

The way I look at things is much more important than how much I see or how much I do not. Whether I see something or I do not, and if someone else sees it, there is no problem; I can learn from the other person. However, both of us must know how we see things. The universe is vast all right, but for me it is only as much as is here within my mind. The more I know, the more I see. By seeing more, I do not solve the problem of facing myself; instead I will be worried about a new problem. The new problem is the stars are decaying and so is our sun. A few billion years from now, there will be no sun. I have a new problem.

The 'I' includes my wishes, my understanding of myself, of the society, of the system, of the current notions that I subscribe to, either consciously or unconsciously. In other words I am the very process of my thinking. I am a product of the society I live in. Naturally I am influenced by its values.

I have seen how these values have changed in the past few years. Our wedding invitations reflect these changes. The invitation I received years ago, carried a line invoking the blessings of Bhagavān, the *ācārya, guru,* followed by the names of the bride and bridegroom and their parents. The *guru*'s permission is mandatory; one cannot marry without the express permission of the *guru*. It is a Vedic injunction that one should not marry until one has paid one's dues to the *guru* and taken his permission, *ācāryāya priyaṁ dhanam āhṛtya prajātantuṁ mā vyavacchetsīḥ*.[4] However, nowadays, I do not see that line. Instead the names of the people who invite for the marriage are there to begin with. Then I read the name of the bridegroom with his qualifications and his job details (with designation) and so on. Nobody marries a qualification, much less a designation. The reason is merely to point out the earning potential of the bride or the groom. Our way of looking at things has changed. The mother of the bride shamelessly informs me that her son-in-law earns four thousand rupees officially and much more unofficially, implying bribes. If it is the accepted norm, that is one thing, but the mother telling me, the *guru*? It is definitely a cognitive change, but for the worse. The change has made her shameless enough to speak about bribes to me. It is decadence. I call this karmic decadence. We know that people are immoral, but we cannot

---

[4] Having offered adequate *dakṣiṇā*, money to the *guru* (for the knowledge received) may one not break the line of progeny (*Taittirīyopanisad* 1.11.1).

boast about it. We cannot talk as though it is normal, as though it is an ordinary, routine affair. We have trivialised such things. It is an unfortunate change in our understanding. Therefore, there is a need to change it.

Cognitive change is the solution for our problems

Modern society has created certain problems for which you do not know whether even psychology has answers. Psychology itself has its own problems; it makes you move in circles without a solution in sight. Therefore, you need to undergo a total change in terms of your vision about yourself, of the world, of your value structure, and of the various notions that are floating around that influence you. This change is purely cognitive. When I say it is cognitive, it means you see it; you see the truth of it. This is exactly the change that we need.

Vedanta brings about the cognitive change

Like psychology, Vedanta is a body of teaching that is meant to bring about a cognitive change. These are the two main disciplines, if I can use the word 'discipline,' which are struggling to bring about cognitive changes. Of course, people have to subject themselves to these changes. Even for that a cognitive change is necessary. It needs a cognitive change to know that one needs a cognitive change. I have met people, who have been listening to my talks and attending classes, trying hard to become Brahman. They definitely need a cognitive change.

We are in for different levels of change that we all need. Please understand this change is instant. It is our seeing. There may be some changes that we see, and we see them cognitively. Some of them may be those we have been already alert to, alive to. They may be habits or our own background psychology. They may be contradicted in life. What can we do to handle such situations?

I would like to bring about this vision in areas where a change is important, so that we can free ourselves from the various notions that bother us. Sometimes we commit a mistake which later proves to be a blessing. But notions are not like that; none of them is a blessing. Each one of them is a bug in the software of our mind. It is better to be rid of it.

In the 17th century, there was a cognitive change, a major breakthrough, in terms of understanding the human body-mind-sense complex and the external, physical world. The world-view changed. The unfortunate aspect of this, however, was that the religious theologies which were interpretations of great masters, did not keep pace with the changes. When it was discovered that the earth is a sphere, it revolves around the sun, and the sun does not move, it was a breakthrough for humanity. Perhaps the people in this country, of this culture, the Vedic culture, knew it all along, if some of their statements are any indication. The nations in West were against the person who discovered this fact and proved it. It is only when the people who matter, see what is being said and change their vision, that the general public changes its vision.

Yet it took centuries for the theologians to accept the new breakthrough, simply because people refused to change cognitively. Progression is always in leaps. It is a jump from one arena to another dimension.

RELIGIOUS LIFE IS INADEQUATE TO SOLVE THE PROBLEMS OF MODERN SOCIETY

I find that religious life does not adequately address the problems of modern society. Once upon a time when life was not that complex, there was no competition. It was true of all societies, of all cultures, but more particularly of Indian society. Professional skills were passed down from father to son. The son of a carpenter, a smith or a craftsman grew to become another carpenter, smith or craftsman. In time, it became a community with a given set of customs and practices. A son of a carpenter often married the daughter of a carpenter and the tradition carried on. It is amazing how, through the generations, the tradition passed on in an unbroken line. Whether it is right or wrong, is not my area of examination. I cite it to show that it provided an infrastructure of least competition, a social infrastructure, which gave some emotional stability. There was a degree of contentment and inner leisure which was good enough for a person to pursue a life of *dharma*. When there is no inner pressure, a life of *dharma* becomes easy. People were ambitious, perhaps, but not greedy. Therefore, people could conform to the common norms necessary for human interaction, the norms, which we call *dharma* and *adharma* in general. They could also conform to the *viśeṣa-dharma*, norms that are conventional, that are cultural, and those that are purely national or legal. They could conform to them without any great sense of loss or compromise.

Today, however, there is an inner pressure to prove ourselves to be somebody; an inner pressure created by our own desires which are one of the privileges of a human being. We require a cognitive change in all these areas. These desires do not remain as mere expressions of human freedom but they become the dictating factors of our lifestyle, our means of achieving the desired ends. The desired ends, themselves, become very important; so important that the means, the rightness of the means, their appropriateness and propriety are not taken into consideration; they are flouted. The attitude is, as long as we can get away with it, anything is acceptable. Life has become a rat race where winning is everything. Consequently, the capacity, the privilege to desire itself becomes the basis for compromise, for the tendency to compromise the norms of *dharma*. A religious life that was once adequate for our forefathers is not enough for the modern man who comes from a background of competition giving way to complexes. We need to change cognitively to understand that mere religion is not going to solve the problem. It has not solved and it will never solve.

Religion has to be more than a set of non-verifiable beliefs

Religion without spirituality, without understanding the spiritual element in it, is not sufficient. A spiritual life, on the contrary, is very important, although there is not much difference between a mature religious life and a spiritual life, really speaking. But there is an obvious difference if our understanding of religion is only a set of beliefs. Religion is called faith in English because there is nothing beyond faith. Every religion has a set of beliefs, all of which are non-verifiable. The goal that they propound is not something that we can attain here. It is a religious goal and that goal is heaven. This, again, is a non-verifiable belief. If heaven is the religious goal, we can believe in it even though it is non-verifiable. Non-verifiable means we cannot verify either its existence or non-existence. Further, the one who believes and the one who does not are both believers. The belief that we will survive death is non-verifiable because at this stage we cannot verify it. Suppose I say, "Yesterday I returned from heaven," you may believe me, but it is also a non-verifiable belief. There will be people to believe. There are always people around to believe anything. It is not the point. The point is people need a cognitive change in all these areas.

When you believe something, you have every right to your belief, but what you believe must be believable. The existence of heaven is believable because you cannot prove that it does not exist. It is not a question of your interest in heaven or not, which is entirely different. That heaven exists and that you will survive death, both these concepts you can believe. When someone asks you to follow him in order to reach heaven, and another person also says the same, whom should you believe? Here lies the problem. Should you choose the one who has better communication skills, or the other because of better packaging, better window dressing? However, neither of them are sure of what they are talking about, yet both of them argue and fight. It makes me wonder. There are many possibilities. Both may be right or wrong, or one may be right and the other wrong. Why is it that people do not see the contradictions? Why people turn into fanatics on the basis of these kinds of beliefs? How do they go about converting people on this basis? When beliefs are basically non-verifiable and can be either right or wrong, with what certainty they ask people to follow them? I cannot understand it at all. This is where I feel a cognitive change is so important. Simple things have to be understood. There will be peace and perhaps a better intellectual climate in the society. As more people begin to think, at least the people who count, there will definitely be a great change.

A simple religious life based on a set of beliefs has yet another belief which is the existence of God. There are others who declare that there is no God. I should like to ask such a person of which God is he or she talking about? This is where a cognitive change is necessary. One has to realise that one is dismissing one's own concept of God. One first understands God in a certain way, and then concludes it cannot be God. Simple form of religion, religious beliefs were, at one time, sufficient since people were not as complex as they are today. Their needs were simple and they could get something out of life, following these beliefs.

The same cannot be said of today. Religion has to be more than a set of non-verifiable beliefs. It is an important area that requires a cognitive change.

Talk 3

Dealing with anger

Today, thanks to technology, life is far easier, smoother, externally. But in the process of technological progress, the inner world, the mind, has become very complex. The single contributory factor to this complexity is the competition when you were a child, when you were not ready to handle it. Like a matured adult if you were equipped to handle competition, then there would be no problem. You would be reasonable because you would not have opinions or judgement about yourself. One of the greatest cognitive breakthroughs of the modern century, born of certain psychological phenomena, is the discovery and the recognition of the unconscious.

What is unconscious?

There is unconscious. In our *śāstra*, we have a word *kaṣāya* that is an equivalent to unconscious. It is not *saṁskāra*, but *kaṣāya*. Our forefathers had an unconscious, but it was not discussed or analysed in detail, probably because it was not such a problem as it is today. The unconscious builds up in the first five years or so, in a human being's life. Granted by *prakṛti*, nature, the unconscious becomes necessary only where there is self-consciousness. In the body-mind-sense complex of an animal, there is external consciousness with certain degree of internal consciousness such as being aware of hunger and thirst.

But the animal does not have self consciousness. Without self-consciousness, there is no self-judgement or complexes. So an animal has no complexes or opinions about itself. It does not complain about its body, its mind or its lot in life. It does not want to be different. A human being, on the contrary, is the most self-conscious of organisms on earth. Consequently, he or she is also psychologically the most complex. Bhagavān has endowed the self-conscious human child the unconscious to help it to survive. He has given the child an extraordinary capacity to push its pain inside to form the other side of the ego, the flip side. The child picks up pain while comparing itself with others, in terms of talent, skill and even colour; there are a variety of problems. The child cannot handle them, but it has to. So, every time there is pain, the child uses this capacity to flip and its unconscious gets loaded. Please understand this well. The unconscious does not mean it is away from your ego. It is your own ego. It is a part of the person. It is just you, except that you are not conscious of it.

Build up of the unconscious

It does not take much to build up the unconscious in a child. If we look at a few common incidents, we can understand this better. There are many homes where the rule of the house is, "Do not cry." When the child cries, the parent chides, "Do not cry. Did I not tell you not to cry?" The child stops crying. Perhaps it will even laugh. The child has just pushed its hurt inside. The mother has a sense of achievement. Had she allowed the child to cry, it would have been better. Earlier, we had joint families where the grandmothers often took the place of a therapist for the child. The child would run to the grandmother and she would console the child. It was very simple. All that she had to do was to comfort the child and say that it was not to blame and that the blame was entirely the mother's. With someone to listen and an empty lap for comfort, nothing was kept inside. The hurt feelings went out. The child's feelings were validated. There was no serious build up of the unconscious which is why our forefathers were better off. With all our accomplishments, academic achievements, technology, money and power, we are emotionally distraught. This is what our society has been reduced to. The children have no one to run to for comfort. When they suddenly laugh, it only means that there is one more reason to load the unconscious. Hurt-by-hurt, the unconscious gets encrusted, and by the time the child is five or six years old, there is already a core person with lot of pain inside.

In the eyes of a child, its parents are infallible. It has to believe that they are. It has no choice because it is completely helpless. I have spoken on this topic many times, and I continue to talk on the subject because it is so important for the parents to understand their responsibility in handling a child. A human child is born totally helpless and this total helplessness is compensated by total trust. Total trust means there has to be infallibility. Although the trust is part of Īśvara's order to help the child to survive, it also becomes a source of pain and hurt. Any action on the part of the parent, conscious or otherwise, if it breaks the child's trust, causes pain. Unable to handle the pain, the child pushes the hurt inside, creating an unconscious. Parents hurt the child by their mechanical actions. For instance, even if one parent is not available to the child, it becomes insecure and is hurt. Though there are reasons for the parents' absence, the child cannot understand and it gets hurt. If there is friction between the parents, if the parents do not keep their promises to the child, if they compare the child with another, insult the child, the list is endless; each of these action hurts the child. And this hurt, in turn, loads the unconscious.

The child looks upon its parents as infallible which they are not. Nobody is infallible. Infallibility is only from the standpoint of the child. The father falls ill, says sorry. He is fallible. He says he will bring a gift for the child's birthday but he forgets; in the child's eyes he becomes fallible. In the process, the child's capacity to trust is eroded. It is further eroded by changes in modern society. A child is warned not to trust strangers. Who are these strangers? Are grandparents, who visit the family, strangers because they do not live with them? It means that in a nuclear family situation, except for the mother and father, everyone is a stranger. Societal rules and behaviour have changed to such an extent that children need to be warned. I say this is sickness. Such rules continually erode the child's capacity to trust. The erosion is a tremendous loss for the individual and for society as a whole. It further reinforces the sense of distrust that already exists in modern society. This is another area where we require a cognitive change to understand that no one is infallible.

Generally, we relate to God as the infallible. Yet our concept of God is such that he is fallible. There was a girl who wanted to marry someone she loved. She prayed to Lord Gaṇeśa but circumstances prevented her from marrying the boy. She writes to me that she has lost faith in God because he did not grant her wish. We require a cognitive change.

The old theological concept of God in heaven showering gifts, needs to be dispensed with. Your concept of God should be proper. You have to replace the God who sits up there, who rewards you if you praise him and punishes if you do not. Simple concept of God is not going to work. It does not work in the schoolroom, much less will it work in freeing yourself from the hold of the unconscious. You have to understand what God is. The whole concept has to undergo change.

Need for understanding and care in bringing up a child

A cognitive change is necessary in bringing up a child in today's world. You are building up an unconscious here. You have to recognise the fact. You have no business bringing a child into the world, if you do not have time to take care of him or her. A child is precious. It is a human child, a self-conscious being, and it picks up pain easily. Any kind of rejection will make the child blame itself which is why everyone has so much inner pressure to prove how good he or she is. In their anxiety to prove, they cross the line of *dharma* and *adharma*. In time, such actions make them coarse and even shameless. These situations are avoidable if only the child is taken care of, either at home or at school, through proper counselling. In fact there should be as many counsellors as teachers; teaching alone is not enough. The counsellors themselves should be first counselled properly.

If we had a proper and adequate counselling system, we could empty the prisons. This is *satyam*. There are no criminals born in the world, only innocent children, but we make criminals out of them. Have we ever asked ourselves why people tend to commit crimes? It is because of anger, anger towards the infallible. People become atheists not because they do not believe in God; it is because they are angry with their father. It is sheer anger towards the father; it is the unconscious that expresses itself. It is a problem due to disapproval of his or her father. Perhaps the father was not kind or attentive enough, and the child felt the father, its God, had failed him or her. This is the person who can become an atheist.

I do not say that every person who is angry with his or her father is going to be an atheist. It is not true. But any one who is an atheist is angry with his or her father. This is *satyam*. Anger towards parents can also result in multiple personality disorders. A habitual offender suffers from this disorder. He is not aware that he commits the same mistake again and again. He is multiple personality which stems from his unconscious. A cognitive change is necessary in all these areas. People are ignorant and suffer unnecessarily. The whole society is victimised because of ignorance.

It is its own victim. People who are supposed to know, do not really know; even teachers are not exceptions. Without proper counselling, the unconscious controls a person's entire life.

Anger is always from the unconscious

Suppose I ask all of you to clap. (Audience clap). You clapped. Some clapped, some of you are in the process of clapping, while some others clapped once, twice or three times. Well, you had the freedom to clap, not to clap, and clap the way you did. I make one more request, "Please be angry for half a minute, come on. Be angry for half a minute." You cannot be angry, is that true? Does it mean that you cannot get angry? It is not true. What does it mean? It means you cannot decide to be angry. You cannot consciously be angry, implying that anger is from unconscious; it is always from the unconscious. Anger comes from within; it is the other side of the ego. All you need is a trigger to let it out.

You have your own erroneous zone, your area of vulnerability. If someone treads on it, well, you react and get angry to the quick. To make matters worse, people advise you, "Please don't be angry." It is a problem due to lack of understanding, lack of awareness of the problem. How can you help a person who is angry? You can help by saying to the person that he or she is angry, but not consciously, and that the anger is due to his or her unconscious. Such a statement makes you non-judgemental and the angry person will not take offence. Religious people constantly advise, "You should not get angry. *Kāma eṣaḥ krodha eṣaḥ rajo-guṇa-samudbhavaḥ.*[5] *Kāma,* desire and *krodha,* anger continually rise in you from *rajo-guṇa.* They are *mahāśana,* voracious, causing you to do wrong actions. Anger incites you to all kinds of unbecoming actions. Therefore you should not get angry." You already know this. Such advice is unwarranted. You do not need such advice. If a religious person should come and tell you, "Do not get angry," you ask him or her, "Please help me get rid of anger."

The unconscious causes anger. It is the child within, the innocent child. It is the expression of the pain inside, which over time has built up into anger. Since the rules at home prevented its expression, the pent up emotions, the unconscious, all come out now and, believe me, they will continue to come out until you are ninety years old! Do not think you can wish them away. Time cannot erase them. So a cognitive change is necessary. You need to be aware of the fact that anger is caused by the unconscious.

There is a reason for anger and it is valid for you to be angry. Perhaps, if I were in your position, I too would be angry. It is a psychological fact. It is science. When you touch fire it is not responsible for burning your finger; its nature is to burn. It is law. So too, anger and the unconscious is also law, the law of psychology. This unconscious is the greatest breakthrough in psychological understanding because there is a need, a necessity for this

---

[5] *Bhagavad Gītā* 3.37

breakthrough in modern society. Every time there is a breakthrough, it is because the paradigms have either shifted or gone altogether.

Processing the Anger Cognitively

People often react inappropriately to a situation. Why this tumult? Why this outburst? It is not necessary. It can be handled more objectively, pragmatically. Great thinkers like Freud and Jung came up with clear understanding of the entire process of the unconscious building up. They could give us the psychological laws from observed behaviour patterns of people with certain common background. So when we view a human emotion like anger from the standpoint of these background laws, the emotion is valid and also unavoidable. Therefore to say, "Don't get angry," is wrong. But there is a caveat; you should neither be a victim of another's anger, nor should another be a victim of your anger.

If you have this cognitive change that there is unconscious, acknowledge it. Acknowledging reality itself is cognitive change. You see the reality and immediately acknowledge, recognise that this is how it is. I tend to be afraid, jealous, restless, competitive. I want to be successful. This is reality. It is a way of handling it. What does success mean to you? There again, you need a cognitive change. I chose the title of this series of talks as, 'Need for cognitive change,' deliberately. I use the word 'need' because you need to change. You need not suffer, and you need not make others suffer.

Please understand, anger never pays. You may think you can get things done through anger. Remember, nobody does things for your anger. If anybody does, it is out of fear for his or her job. You are such an angry person that you may even fire them. Therefore, it is not anger that gets things done. You can definitely achieve your purpose differently. All it needs is a cognitive change on your part. The first cognitive change is, anger does not pay. Second, you can be pleasant and still get things done. To be strict is different from being angry. I do not say that you should not get angry. I say you need to process your anger. Your anger can be processed. It is only a symptom of your pain. You can get help in processing your anger by empowering your spouse and children. You can tell them, "I am angry now. I will talk to you later." We call it *dama* in Sanskrit. It means you do not follow through your anger with words or actions. You pull down the shutters as it were by saying you will talk later. If the other person is angry, you can tell him or her, "You are angry now. Let us talk later."

Nobody has a right to make you a victim of his or her anger. It is a human being's right to retain his or her dignity. You can say things pleasantly without shouting, without evoking the other person's defence mechanisms. You can transform your house into a home from now on. You cannot give a better gift to your child than this insight, this great insight. You are not judged in the process. Even an angry person is not judged. You accept his or her anger.

When we speak in anger, there is heat and no light. We are told that the presiding deity of the organ of speech, *vāk*, is fire.

Fire has two attributes; one is heat and the other, light. When we speak, more often it is heat that comes out, there is no light at all, even though speech is meant to throw some light. Let us avoid heated exchanges; this is called *dama*. It is a cognitive change on our part to understand that anger is natural and there is a reason for anger. What is inappropriate is not anger or talking about anger, but talking or doing things in anger.

The problem is when you are already angry, you will be fuming inside. If you do not process that anger, there will be no *śama*. *Śama* means resolution of anger. If you do not resolve anger and you have not expressed yourself, it amounts to suppression which brings further complications. You need to express anger appropriately. You can write out your anger. Write your feelings in a language you are at home with. Write all that you wanted to say, wanted to do, but could not. You could also shout it out, at a beach or a park, when you are alone. It is an appropriate expression of anger because no one is victimised. This is how you change.

In the recognition of the unconscious, you do not blame yourself. No child is responsible for all that has happened. It is absolutely innocent. It does not mean, however, that the parents are to blame. They have their own unconscious to deal with. There is no need to blame anyone. If they had known a little more, they would have done better. They did not know. Consequently there is pain which manifests as anger. So anger is more an outcome. With this understanding, you can create a home, a functional home, without traces of old problems. There is dialogue. There is honesty and fairness. Even a small hut becomes heaven when there is dialogue, when there is understanding. You can be honest only when there is no shame. You need not be ashamed of anger because you understand, it is not wrong, it is an expression of the unconscious.

In India, there are so many public lectures on religion, behaviour, self-improvement and so on, which makes us believe, not only anger but desires also are wrong. To have desires is considered a problem. People ask me, "Swamiji, I have been studying the *Gītā* and I find that I have too many desires. What should I do? How can I reduce desires?" It is a problem. We need a cognitive change here as much as we need a change in understanding our concept of God.

A CONGNITIVE CHANGE IN OUR CONCEPT OF GOD THAT CAUSES FEAR

A religion or a concept of God that causes fear in any form cannot help a person grow spiritually. Most of the popular religions have a concept of God which spells fear. In the eyes of the mother all her sons, the noble, the accomplished and the one given to alcohol and crime, are the same in terms of care and love. She may be proud of one. She may be in agony thinking about the other. The agony comes from love and care. There should be someone in this world who is more than the mother, who is totally non-judgemental and therefore infallible, the very thought of whom relaxes me, not frightens me. If there is such a being, whether human or conceived as Īśvara, God, that is needed for a human being to get well. The concept of God and the human destination, the ultimate goal, are to be examined and understood. I think a cognitive change in these areas is very, very important if I have to get anything out of religion.

A person who is kept in check in terms of actions that are not accepted as ethical, because of damnation later, because of some fear, may be religious, but I cannot say that the person is, in any way, spiritual. Fear of God is a common expression. If a person is considered God-fearing, it means that he follows some values. It implies that God is someone to be feared. This is to be examined. God loves you but will punish you. It is like the message the children get from their parents mostly. When the father brings a gift for the child, it is an expression of love. When the same person is not available for any dialogue or severely punishes the child for no reason, then he becomes the opposite. The child is confused. The message is, "I love you but do not come anywhere near me." This is a conflicting double message. If the same thing is extended to God who is in heaven then, "He loves you; even though he is far away in heaven. Do not think that you can be away from him. His eyes are all over. He knows exactly what you are doing. If you do not obey him, he will punish you." This is again a double message.

We need to examine the concept of God in heaven, if we are to benefit by it. We can definitely get something from prayers, whether we think of God being in heaven or do not even think of his location. One person said, "I do not know what you are O Lord, but wherever you are and in whichever form, unto you my *namaskāra*."[5] This salutation is from an open-minded objective person. Such an attitude does help. Any religious life does help.

For a person born and brought up in a complex society, mere religious life is not sufficient. You need to change cognitively in your appreciation of what God is. It also means you have to be very clear in terms of what it is that you have to accomplish in your life through this religion.

---

5 *tava tattvaṁ na jānāmi kīdṛśo'si maheśvara. yādṛśo'si mahādeva tādṛśāya namo namaḥ* (*Śivamahimna stotram* 40-41)

Talk 4

Understanding the human goal

The ultimate goal of most religions appears to be going to heaven. Once the goal is not to be accomplished here, naturally it becomes a matter of faith, which is why religions are called faiths. But we cannot say that *vaidīka-dharma* is a faith, even though there are some beliefs in it, such as going to Kailāśa or Vaikuṇṭha after death. We need to examine these concepts. The theology of some of these religions is purely an interpretation of the words of accepted masters, the people who are looked upon as messiahs or sons of God or those who have spoken with God. Their words form the basis for the theology, just as the Vedic words form the basis for varieties of theologies.

A religious belief cannot go against reason

The theologies are imposed upon you, and you are expected to accept them without questions because they are beliefs. You can accept a non-verifiable belief as one. You may not be interested in the belief. But you cannot accept something that goes against your reason or experience, because you do not consider that believable. For instance if I say, there is an elephant outside the auditorium, most of you may believe me. You may grant that I have ESP, extra sensory perception. However, if I say that I have a rose in my hand, and therefore there should be an elephant outside, can you believe me? You cannot because it is absolutely illogical. Even if God says you cannot believe him. You may at best laugh it off by saying he is joking, but you cannot believe him. Therefore, what cannot be believed should not be believed. But you have the freedom to believe or not, which is beyond my verification. If you believe something that is not against your reason, perception or experience, you can be respected for your belief. You have every right to your beliefs. However, it is foolish if you believe something that is not in keeping with your means of knowledge. You need to be very alert to know which of the beliefs are within reason and experience, and which are not.

If heaven is the ultimate goal, you can accept the belief as the stated goal of all theologies. There are certain theologies that insist that having a human body and reaching heaven is a one-time affair. They also say, it is only the human being who has a soul. The rest of creation is meant for human beings to enjoy. It means that the world is meant for human consumption. Such theological concepts unwittingly encourage environmental destruction. You need a cognitive change here.

The trees, animals and the entire creation have a right to live as much as a human being. It requires a different mindset. If, out of this changed mindset, there is environmental concern and care, you can respect it. If environmental concern is only because human life is in peril, then it is pure selfishness. We need to change our way of thinking. The theologies consider that God personally created human beings in his image. The darker side to these theologies is that they leave you with no choice except to follow them. They threaten you with dire consequences if you reject their beliefs. Further, their consequences are eternal, forever, eternal bliss or eternal damnation. If you do not choose heaven, their concept of heaven, then you will have to go to hell. It is an either or situation. They paint such a dark picture of hell, that out of sheer fright, you follow them. How can you believe such concepts? It is against all reason and experience. A mother condones her son for even the worst crimes. Of course she agonises over his behaviour, but it is because of her love for him. Is God then worse than a mother on earth? Therefore, this concept has to undergo a change. In everybody's mind it has to change.

Let me narrate this incident. Once I was in Rochester and there was a television interview. The interviewer had informed his viewers that they were going to see a real live Swami. The real live Swami came; it was a live interview. The interviewer was very hostile to India and all that is Indian. He asked me, "Why are all these American youngsters after Oriental religions?" I said, "Maybe they think they will find some solutions there." I did not say that they had solutions. I said they think they are going to find solutions. It is a very clean answer. Then he said, "Oh, a lot of Indians also come here to follow this religion." I answered, "No, it is not true. Indians come here for jobs. They come here, perhaps, for higher education. They do not come here for religion. They have enough of it there." His next question was, "Why is India overpopulated?"

The whole build up was very hostile. The interviewer was very hostile in the tone of his voice; the demeanour, everything, and then he posed this question on population. I never thought about it before. I know that India is overpopulated, but I never thought about it the way I answered. The answer came just shooting out of my mouth.

I said, "It is because we did not occupy North America, we did not occupy South America, we did not occupy Australia, we did not occupy New Zealand, we did not occupy Rhodesia, we did not occupy South Africa, we did not occupy Hawaii. Let all these people go back to Europe and England, let me see whether they have got a place to put their toes on." (Applause).

The person then calmed down and asked me, "Swami, generally what type of questions do people ask you?" You better believe me when I say that I asked some questions to myself and answered them. It is a true incident. It is *satyam*. Do you know why it is so? It is because we believe in non-encroachment; it is our *dharma*. We do not encroach on others' land. We do not encroach on others' religion and culture. The one who encroaches is an *ātatāyin*, and such a crime attracts capital punishment according to our *dharma-śāstra*.

Conversion hurts the core person

Converting another person into your religion is a form of *hiṁsā*, harm. Perhaps it is the worst *hiṁsā* because the religious person is at the core of every human being.

There are many forms of *hiṁsā*. Forcing people to accept concepts out of fear is *hiṁsā*. The father is a role; the son is a role. But the core person is one who is related to the Lord, which why religious sentiments are always very sensitive issues. When you convert a person from one religion to another without realising the damage you cause, you are hurting not just the individual but also the family, in fact, the whole society. We cannot tread upon a religious sentiment; it is hurt and it is wrong. What is wrong has to be understood as such. This is what I mean by cognitive change. You cannot stand on my toes, hurt me and then invite me for a dialogue. I can discuss only when you stop hurting me.

You can change only if you have a value for change, and that happens only when your concept of the ultimate goal changes; when your concept of God changes. The goal cannot be from a scripture; it has to come from you. The concept that you have to return to heaven after being placed on earth by God is laughable. It raises more questions than it solves. Such a concept makes God a sadist who deliberately wants people to suffer. It does not make any sense whatsoever.

As a human being, you are endowed with the faculty of choice, of freewill. You have to exercise it. You have to live intelligently. You have no choice but to choose. Therefore, you have to examine the various concepts available to you and choose. If fear is the reason for choice, then as long as there is fear in the heart of a human being, there can be no spirituality. The cause of fear is the judgemental person. A day will come when God will sit and judge. Anyone who is judgemental is mental. It reflects a 'holier than thou' attitude which is not a healthy attitude. You can accept a human being with such frailties, but you cannot think of God in the same way.

Concept of heaven in Indian scriptures

Indian scriptural books also mention heaven as an achievable end. The difference is you go to heaven for your good deeds, as a result of your *karma*. The other religions also state that you will stay in heaven for a period of time and then return. It is not an eternal heaven. There cannot be an eternal heaven simply because eternity cannot begin. Eternity is not within time. It is something that is, was and shall ever be, in the same form. There cannot be a change. If at time T1 it is in one form, at time T2 it is in another, it is subject to time, and therefore non-eternal. If this is the meaning of eternal, where is the question of an eternal heaven? It is completely illogical and hence unacceptable.

On the other hand, if you say you will be in heaven for some time, but return once your *karma* is exhausted, I can accept that because it is reasonable. Being a belief, I can neither prove nor disprove it, but it has some logic that is acceptable.

Anything that I see in the Veda, I find, I cannot raise my voice against because it is reasonable all the way. It does not want me to blindly follow its words. It wants me to believe few concepts and understand certain others. I need a cognitive change here. I need to know what is to be believed and what is to be understood. It is an area of great confusion. Often, I question what is to be believed and swallow what is to be understood. If a person says that he believes God is everywhere, it not a question of belief, it is something to be understood. Next, he questions the concept of rebirth and asks for proof and so on. He does not realise it is a matter for belief. So, the difference has to be very clearly understood.

Religious life versus spiritual life

Picking up the thread again, the concept of an eternal heaven is not acceptable. Anyone who chooses to go to heaven out of fear of hell, cannot be a spiritual person. At best, he can lead a religious life. A spiritual person will not be a fanatic much less be one who is subject to fear. A spiritual person is someone who is free from fear, who can accommodate everybody, who has compassion, and who will not hurt another. There cannot be spirituality as long as there is no consideration for others' sentiments. A spiritual person is one who wants to get rid of fear, to get rid of varieties of greed and so on, who does not blame a devil or an external force, and who is able to address his or her problems. A religious person need not address these. He can be angry, he can be jealous, hateful, and yet be religious. He can also earn money through various means and give one percent to Parameśvara. He can do that. We can say at least he gives charity because he has some *śraddhā*. A religious person need not change, he does not change. A religious life is not spiritual life but a spiritual life implies religious life. Please understand the difference.

You cannot make any headway in a spiritual life without religion. Being spiritual means you neither blame yourself nor others, you address your problems. It is the beginning of spiritual life. It gains power, motivation and perseverance only because whatever you seek or want as the goal, rises from you. You are the solution to the problem. You should decide your goal, not a scripture or another special person.

The problem of a human being is facing oneself. When you suddenly start singing, it is not because you are very happy or you love music. You sing because you want to divert yourself from some remembered shame or hurt. You divert yourself from facing the problem. Whenever you recall a shameful incident, everyone has a few of them, you are ashamed and music will be the next step. The latest popular song will be on your lips. You cannot face yourself. You cannot stand your shame, not even its memory. Change starts from here.

One is wanting in all ways

There is a sense of want, a sense of limitation in you. It forms the basis of your struggle in life. The solution that you seek in terms of getting, achieving, or getting ahead of another, is centred on yourself. The limitation is centred on you alone.

As a wanting person, whatever you do, whatever you get or achieve, cannot make you free from being a wanting you. What you seek is not an object, but freedom from being a wanting person. The freedom that you seek has to be centred on yourself.

If, in reality, you are a limited person, you have no solution. You will remain limited forever. If you are identified with your body, definitely you are limited because the body is subject to age, time and place. If you identify yourself with your mind, then that is also limited. Emotionally you are limited and a wanting person; being cheerful is an impossibility. Knowledge-wise, you are limited. Your knowledge extends only up to the next question. You know an object as a flower, a rose, its colour, but you do not know the reason for its colour. Even in the human body and its functions, there are large areas where your knowledge is wanting. Memory-wise, the limitation is proverbial. You remember each hurt and pain very well. Occasionally, of course, you do recall some of the good times you have had. Thus, you find that memory-wise also you are wanting. So in terms of knowledge, desires, emotions, condition of the mind, health, height, looks, money, friendship, my God in everything we are wanting. If this is who we are, we are booked. We are booked forever.

THE URGE TO BE FREE BEING NATURAL HAS A MEANS OF FULFILMENT HERE

The urge to be free from want is natural. If the urge is natural, like hunger or thirst, it means there should be a means for fulfilling that urge. If these natural urges can be fulfilled, then the problem of my being a wanting person must also have a solution. This problem is not peculiar to me as a person, as an individual; I find that it is universal. It exists only in highly evolved self-conscious life forms such as human beings. It is not evident in other life forms. I am self-conscious, but in that very self-consciousness, the conclusion that I am limited, wanting, insignificant and so on, is unacceptable. Just as hunger and thirst have a solution, my sense of limitation is unacceptable because it has a solution. I have an insight that is acceptable to myself. There is a solution. Who is the solution? I am the sloution. If I am wanting, then I am the problem to myself. The problem that I am a wanting person is a spiritual problem that is common to all. It has nothing to do with going to heaven and other similar concepts. It is a problem here and now. It exists because I am a self-conscious person and the solution has to be found here.

To say this is how life on earth will be, but once we go to heaven, all our problems will be resolved, is merely a palliative. It is purely a belief, and we have to reconcile the unacceptable fact of remaining a wanting, discontented person. Travelling to heaven and other similar concepts are religious tourism, really speaking. If there is going to be a future birth, it implies that there was a previous birth and a birth previous to it, and another before that, and so on to infinite regression. Every *jīva* is a tourist. We have travelled a lot, and now we are here trapped in this body. We need a cognitive change here. It is called *vyavasāyātmikā buddhiḥ, niscayātmikā buddhiḥ,* wherein there is clarity with reference to what we truly want. It has to be recognised.

THE URGE TO BE FREE IS FULFILLED BY THE KNOWLEDGE 'I AM HAPPINESS'

The solution lies right here, in changing my understanding of myself. Perhaps what I think I am is wrong. There must be a reason for my wrong thinking. There is a basis for questioning my thinking because, in spite of being a wanting person, I am able to laugh, find moments of happiness. The two are opposed to each other, the wanting me and the happy me. How can they coexist at the same time and place? It is impossible. Despite the problems of limitation, everybody is happy now and then. Why? It appears to me that there is no rule that I should fulfil all my wants to be happy. It means I can be happy without fulfilling any want. I can be happy in this body, mind, and intellect, despite my wanting them to be different. If it is so, perhaps I am the very happiness I am seeking. My God, if it is true, I can be happy without fulfilling any desires!

There are people who, despite their exposure to this kind of teaching, think that only if they fulfil a desire, they become happy. But that happiness does not last in the wake of another desire. They conclude that real happiness lies between the fulfilled desire and the rise of another desire. There is some truth in this statement, but it is not the whole truth. Sometimes you fulfil a desire and wish you were never born. Sometimes you do not fulfil a desire and yet you are happy. You find that you are happy without a particular reason.

Once, I read a hoarding in Mumbai, "Why is a Standard Battery like a mother-in-law?" Below the question was the answer, "Because it goes on and on and on." (Laugther).

You laughed all right, but did you fulfil a desire? No. Your tenant has not moved away from your house. You have a credit card, but it is over the limit; you have not yet paid your dues. Your mother-in-law continues to be the same. She has not changed, even though she sometimes attends Vedanta classes. Yet you laugh. Why? It is because you do not need to fulfil all your desires to be happy.

Happiness is your very nature. You have to change cognitively. You have to be what you are; only then everything becomes a plus for you. You have to discover freedom from the sense of limitation which is centred on yourself. If you are the problem, you are the solution. This cognitive change will put everything in perspective in your life. You need not change your life pattern, your lifestyle, your ambitions and so on.

If you are what you want to be, then your vision of God also has to be different, because God has no more contribution to make in your life. You have to see what that God is, because there is confusion in your understanding. The concept of God has to undergo a change.

Talk 5

An analysis of the concept of God

In general, people accept the existence of a higher force, a force they consider as infallible but the problem is they search for the infallible.

The human child trusts its parents as infallible. The capacity to trust is given to the human child as a sheer necessity. Until it was born, it was part of the mother; it was secure, complete. Once it leaves this security at birth, it starts an independent life without being equipped to handle the independence. Naturally, it is a frightened organism, struggling to live. The human child cannot cope with fear which is why it trusts the people who take care of it. When the child is small and insignificant, given to all the elements and forces, its sanity entirely depends upon its capacity to trust. Being fragile and incapable of survival, it has to trust and it trusts. The trust must be total in order for it to feel safe and secure. The parents are infallible until the child grows to discern, to see that they are fallible. They fall ill and that is fallibility. Therefore every human child is bound to discover that the parents are fallible. If death occurs the fallibility is devastatingly discovered. Later, all through its life, the child seeks the infallible. It is another way of looking at God, as the infallible.

Need for the infallible

In every tribe there is an equal to God who is supposed to be the infallible. It is a sheer necessity both for survival and for sanity. In China, when Mao introduced communism, which dismissed all the religions and religious forms as rubbish, he introduced a book, the famous Red Book, which became an object of worship. The people were made to think that the Red Book would solve all problems. They began worshipping that book. The human heart has a need for the infallible.

Concept of God has to undergo a change

The concept of the almighty, omniscient, omnipresent, infallible God includes looking upon him as a source of blessing and punishment, and who is to be propitiated by rites and rituals. God as the source of both punishment and blessing is a primitive concept. It was adequate for people leading a simple life, who did not have the complexity of modern society. Today, it is an environment of competition. The parents themselves are products of a competitive society, having experienced success and failure. It is a neurotic environment and the child acquires more complexes than it did a century ago. The primitive concept of God can no longer provide sanity or security. The concept is inadequate and wrong. It has got to be right in order to bless.

We need to understand very clearly the meaning of infallible. The common understanding is that God is infallible as long as he grants all our wishes and prayers. The moment our wish is denied, God's infallibility is questioned. Once I heard a well known person declare that he no longer believes in God because he lost his wife who was a great devotee of Lord Gaṇeśa. People do not understand the meaning of infallibility. We cannot afford to be ignorant of what is infallible. Infallibility does not mean God should grant all our wishes. This concept has to change. God is to be understood as infallible. It is the truth. It is not mere necessity that we seek the infallible. We need to see this is how God is.

Our ignorance of God has brought humanity sorrow, distress, and even destruction. The fanatics who fight and argue are all ignorant. They are not only ignorant, they refuse to understand, to see reason. Theologies have programmed people not to think. They further emphasise this by declaring that it is God's wish. God does not want you to think; he only wants you to obey. If you think or question, it means your ego, the devil, has taken over and there is no place for God. It is a concept. Theology has made its position so airtight that it does not allow any fresh air, any fresh thought to enter. There is no possibility of change.

I cannot be a hostage in the hands of these theologies any longer. I have to grow out of them or make them more meaningful. A cognitive change is inevitable. If I have to be sane, never mind God-realisation and all that, just to be sane, I cannot afford to be ignorant because I have been given the faculty for knowledge. I have to live my life intelligently. I have no choice. I have to look into the generally accepted concept of God.

The concept of God seated in heaven, in Kailāśa or Vaikuṇṭha, is a prevalent belief. Please understand, I am not criticising any religion but merely examining a popular concept of God. I have discussed this before. The concept of God in heaven throws up a number of issues such as, if God created heaven, where was God before the creation of heaven and so on. The whole edifice of theology just falls apart if I look into these questions. The concept is completely non-believable.

Space and time are part of creation. I cannot afford to be ignorant of these facts. The concept of space and time being absolute in classical physics has collapsed already. The whole paradigm has shifted which is why Einstein cried when he understood the relative nature of space, of time, of everything. He said, "I feel that the ground on which I stand is sinking."

Everything I considered as tangible realities, that realism, has undergone a drastic change. There is nothing solid in this world. At the macro level it is solid, while at the micro level it is just waves and particles. Even that I cannot define until I decide what I want to observe, the speed or position. If I decide to observe the speed, it is a wave, and it is a particle, if I decide to observe its location.

Modern physics has brought about fundamental changes in our view of the world and these changes have to be recognised. A refusal to accept or see these changes, to continue with a mistake against all evidence, reveals a psychological problem. Physicists have proved beyond doubt that the whole thing is collapsible, including the proton, which was thought to be a stable particle. Modern science has understood what we see is not what we think it is. It corroborates the statements of Vedanta.

Vedanta unfolds God as non-separate from creation

Vedanta calls the entire universe a *jagat*. The word has a special meaning, *jāyate gacchati iti jagat*, it is born and it is gone, a continuous stream of born, gone, born, gone. Anything bound by time, which is the entire universe, is subject to change again. If it is so, then you cannot say God was there somewhere before the creation. If there is a creator for the *jagat*, it has to be looked into. If such a creator exists, definitely he cannot be inside the *jagat*. If he cannot be inside, he has to be outside his creation. Words such as 'inside' and 'outside' denote space, and space itself lies within creation. So God cannot be within or outside space, which effectively means space itself is God. Space is not different from or separate from God. We need to examine the old concept of God, the creator, being separate from his creation.

The Veda is the saving grace for modern humanity. To me it looks like we have reached a point where nothing can help us except the teaching of Vedanta, all that is here is only one thing. It appears humanity is driving itself to that inevitable understanding of the wholeness, the oneness of all that is, which we can call universe or creation.

If space is not separate from God, then how did the universe come about? Perhaps, there is no creation at all. Then, how do you explain the world that you live and experience? If you say, as some do, that it is nature and that nature created the world, then is nature intelligent, sentient to create or is it insentient, inanimate? If you offer a prayer to nature, it must be intelligent to accept your prayer. For instance, you do not offer your worship to a wall simply because it cannot accept your worship. So, what do you mean by 'nature?' You cannot accept the insentient nature created the world, because the world is intelligently put together.

Jagat is intelligently put together

Here is an example, I often use, to explain that the world is intelligently put together. Suppose I say, there is a valley in Switzerland where clocks and watches spring up from the ground. Can you believe me ? You cannot. However, I insist it is nature; it is created by nature. You will counter by saying a clock or a watch is created with many different parts put together. They are intelligently put together simply because they are available for knowledge, for study. There is a dial, hour hand, minute hand, mechanical parts and much more. Each part has a specific purpose that reflects the underlying knowledge and know-how. Since it is intelligently assembled, it is a creation, created for a purpose by the human being. A spider's web, a honeycomb, a clockwork toy or a computer microchip, whether a simple crude production or technologically intensive, it is a product of an intelligent being. Not only are they products of an intelligent being, they reveal the skill and the capacity of that intelligent being. It implies both knowledge of what is produced and the ability to produce it. We find that all things here are intelligently put together, be it a leaf, a plant, or a solar system. It implies all-knowledge. The all-knowledge must include all skill because we see the product here. Our human body is an amazing piece of engineering and is obviously put together with great intelligence. It is a talking, walking, living, breathing work of art, alive and intelligently created. Once we accept that all this is intelligently put together, intelligently created, then it is available for our understanding. What is created with knowledge can be studied and analysed. By looking at the computer screen, we can figure out the software involved, and there are wizards in this field. We find the more we study, more the knowledge unfolds.

We have reached a point from where the paradigms have to change. The paradigms separating physiology, biology and all other branches of knowledge have disappeared. We find that one discipline borders on others, be it higher mathematics, nuclear physics or any other field. They had to come together, making the research more and more complex. We cannot understand any phenomenon through just one discipline.

If we take the human body, you find that orthopaedics, physiology, biochemistry, pathology and many more branches of knowledge have come together. Not only have various disciplines of knowledge melded together in a human body, they cannot be improved upon. Imagine if the nose was on top of the head instead of where it is now. We would have to take the coffee or tea above for the flavour, and bring it down to the mouth for taste. As a result, we could end up pouring the drinks down our nose! This would happen every time we wanted to drink something. Fortunately, the nose is positioned perfectly, near the mouth, so that we can get both the aroma and taste in one operation.

We can very well understand how things are intelligently put together and cannot be improved either. In fact Einstein said, the world is as it is because it cannot be otherwise. In contrast, a human creation, no matter how ingenious or brilliant, can be improved upon. An automobile commercial says, "Have you driven a Ford, lately?" The 'lately' is added after a small pause. The same commercial is used year after year, which means they are continually improving. It is human intelligence. It is fallible and can be improved upon by learning from past mistakes.

It is not just the human body; the entire universe is a perfect arrangement. It is a symbiotic whole. I need the trees and animals and they in turn need me. I blow out carbon dioxide, which the trees require, and they give out oxygen, which I require. It is a perfect arrangement. As I study things around me, I discover the intricacy of design, detail, a vast network of knowledge. In other words, I do not see the dividing line between the hardware and the software. Where there is hardware, there is the software too. It is an intelligently assembled organic whole.

Creation presupposes an intelligent cause

In this extraordinary set up, there is no particular person involved. If it is nature, according to some, it is intelligent nature. It is an intelligent creation. I use the word 'creation' provisionally. Creation implies a creator, because of the knowledge involved. Knowledge, in turn, implies an intelligent being since knowledge cannot rest in an inert entity. It has to rest in a conscious being, a being with the knowledge of not one thing or another, but knowledge of everything including all the possibilities within the *jagat*. Knowledge of everything means known and unknown; what is on the surface, what is potential, is all-knowledge. We call this all-knowledge being, Īśvara. We can use the word 'God' without the mindset of God located above.

The all-knowledge, Īśvara or God has no specific location or gender. If we understand that God has no gender, then we can invoke God as he or she. In our culture, God is both he and she. It reveals that our forefathers had a clear understanding of what is Īśvara.

An inquiry into the material for creation

As we continue to inquire into Īśvara, the conscious, all-knowledge being, we will have to pause because the question of material will arise. With what material did Īśvara create the world? There should be a material cause; if there is a maker, the material is inevitable. Mere material cannot create. We do not see it anywhere. Some theologies insist that God created the world out of nothing. The concept is against experience and reason, it is non-believable. This is where *śāstra* comes to our help.

Inquiring into the material for *jagat* with the help of the *śāstra*, we understand that it is from Īśvara alone. The material is not separate from the intelligent cause. God is both the intelligent and the material cause. From the material aspect we can call God a she, and from the maker standpoint, we can call God a he. Kālidāsa says,[6] '*vāgarthau iva sampṛktau...jagataḥ pitarau vande pārvatī-parameśvarau*, I offer my salutation to Pārvatī and Parameśvara, the parents of the creation, who are inseparable, as a word and its meaning.' The concept of identity of the maker and the material cannot be better expressed than this.

You seek infallible parents, and you have in God Ardhanārīśvara, a he and she; one side is male and the other, female. God as Umāmaheśvara or Lakṣmīnārāyaṇa are one and the same. He is he and he is she or she is he; in fact she contains he. Therefore Īśvara as both the maker and material cause is understandable and acceptable. It is not blind faith.

JAGAT IS NON-SEPARATE FROM ĪŚVARA, THE MATERIAL CAUSE

If Īśvara is both the efficient and material cause, what is the relationship between the world, the *jagat*, and the material? Can the world be away from the material? Can a product ever be away from its material? For instance, shirt is a product. Is there a shirt independent of its material? It needs some fabric, silk, cotton or any other. Can you even imagine a shirt without a material? You cannot. In fact, you cannot think of anything in the world without its material. The product and the material are inseparable. Be it gold and chain, clay and pot; where the product is, there is the material.

---

[6] *Raghuvaṁśa* 1.1.

Where the effect is, there is the cause. If God is both the maker and the material, then, where the *jagat* is, there the cause is, God is.

You can understand now that space, time, galaxies, solar systems, sun, stars, planets, everything is God. There is no question of belief here. It is something to be understood. We can prove it. Our *śāstra* does not say that there is no God; neither does it say that there is one God. It says, all that is here is God. Such an understanding is like fresh air for a dying man. It is oxygen to the thinking person, because it opens up our entire vision. We understand what God is; all that is here is God. This vision has to be assimilated. It is not a concept; it is a vision and you have to see clearly, by understanding. It is a vision that opens up avenues for us to resolve our problems, including your understanding of what is infallible.

Jagat is only a manifestation

Once we have the vision, God is both the maker and the material cause, the *jagat* cannot be separate from him, we can now understand the meaning of word *sarva-vyāpin*, the one who is all pervasive. All pervasive does not mean there are two different factors, a *jagat* on one hand, which in turn is pervaded by Īśvara. It means that all that is here is a manifest form of Īśvara. The word 'creation' itself is in question. If we accept the word creation, then the question of the creator, his location, the purpose and so on have to be inquired into. Such a situation does not arise when we see the *jagat* is a manifestation of Īśvara.

Dream model to understand oneness of maker and the material

It is not easy to assimilate the fact that the maker and the material are identical. Using an appropriate model, such as sleep and dream, can help you overcome this difficulty. In sleep your individuality is resolved. You have no idea of space, time, object or the world. You are there, but without a thought of yourself. In Sanskrit the condition during sleep is called *avyākṛta*, undifferentiated. The *upaniṣad*[7] cites an example for the undifferentiated state. If you break the seed of a tree or plant, you do not find anything inside. There is no trace of the tree within the seed, neither trunk, roots, leaves, flowers nor fruit. Yet the seed contains the entire tree in an undifferentiated form. Given the right conditions, the seed grows into the particular tree; it gets differentiated. The potential that lies within the seed is manifest.

You have a similar situation in deep sleep. There is no differentiation, rich, poor, healthy, blind, famous and the not so famous, all are alike in deep sleep. A noted musician forgets his music while asleep, if his snores are an indication. Most certainly, they do not keep to any musical scale. You can say that the person is in an undifferentiated state in deep sleep. He is *avyākṛta*.

You wake up from sleep, not completely, but half awake, the experience is dream state, *svapna*. You see a world similar to the waking world, with similar objects, persons and situations. You are the maker and the material for

---

[7] *Chāndogyopaniṣad* 8.10.1

the dream; the intelligent cause as well as the material cause. In dream, you have created everything out of yourself. An important fact to note here is, you have the knowledge of all that is in your dream. You cannot create an object that is unknown to you. Every object in the dream is always a known object. My favourite '*gagabugain,*' you cannot create because neither you nor I know what '*gagabugain*' is. Any object that you see in your dream has to be taken from you, from your memory, because it is your projection. For the dream creation, you are the knowledgeable person with the necessary software. You are the intelligence for the dream. Even if you see a man with horns, it is from your memory of a cartoon or a science fiction movie. It is your knowledge that is both the software and the hardware for the dream. No other example can help you understand the fact of the maker and the material being identical as clearly as the dream example. If you understand this, then it is not difficult for you to understand that in deep sleep your individuality is *avyākṛta,* undifferentiated, unmanifest.

There is so much knowledge involved in the dream creation itself. You are the maker and the material, one inseparable whole. It is the truth and truth means reality. It requires a cognitive change to know that there cannot be many truths, many realities. There can be many theologies for want of proper knowledge. Where knowledge of an object or a fact is involved, there cannot be differences. A rose is a rose; there cannot be different opinions about it. You can at best say 'rose' in different languages. You cannot say that it is a rabbit or a mango. Suppose I show you a pot and say, "Look at this apple, this red apple." You cannot believe me.

You may give me the benefit of doubt and think that I am joking, but you will not believe me. If I continue in the same vein, then you will begin to pity me thinking that something has happened to the poor Swami. Knowledge is not subject to doubt, *vikalpa*. You can know more about an object, but you cannot know it differently. You can continue exploring a rose plant until you reduce it to particles. This is the only choice you have regarding knowledge. With regard to non-verifiable beliefs, you can concede someone the freedom to hold on to them. A belief that goes against reason and experience, is no longer a belief; it is an error, a mistake.

Like an object that collapses into its material, there is a cosmic collapse, called *pralaya*. I deliberately use the word 'collapse' because nothing is really destroyed. The word '*saṁhāra*' does not mean destruction; it is resolution, resolving into the causal form, like a destroyed pot resolves into clay. What is differentiated becomes less, until it finally resolves into the causal state, *avyākṛta*, which is Īśvara. From the causal state, again, it manifests, differentiates, and it is Īśvara manifest in this form. Īśvara alone, who is all-knowledge, manifests in the form of space, time and so on.

To understand the total manifestation as Īśvara, and nothing is outside Īśvara, the *śāstra* employs a model of five subtle and gross elements—space, air, fire, water and earth. You have to understand it as a model. The intention of the *śāstra* is not to prove any creation or process. It just wants you to understand all that is here is Īśvara.

TALK 6

ĪŚVARA IS ONE MAHĀ ORDER

The all-knowledge that is Īśvara is manifest in the form of the *jagat*, known and unknown to you; it includes your body, mind, senses and your unconscious. If this is clear, let us look at this *jagat*, a manifestation of Īśvara, in a different way. We can understand the various things in the world either as discrete objects or as systems, as order.

ĪŚVARA AS PHYSICAL ORDER

The entire physical universe consists of galaxies, nebulae and so on. The galaxies are moving away from each other; we call it as the expanding universe. It is not that the universe is expanding and moving the galaxies away. The whole universe is looked upon as certain cosmological or physical order. It consists of phenomena not only like the sun and the stars, but also, forces, varieties of forces from gravitation onwards. We can look at all these as one order, a physical order. In Sanskrit we call it *niyati, bhūta-bhautika-niyati,* the order of elements and elementals.

ĪŚVARA AS BIOLOGICAL ORDER

Given this vast universe with its numerous galaxies, with life forms on earth, there must be the possibility of life elsewhere , in other systems. The study of life and the various life sciences are part of the extensive biological order. If the Darwinian theory of evolution is true, it is included in that order. When you study a given subject matter such as botany or microbiology, you are exploring the biological system in general. We call this common order or system as *samaṣṭi*. The biological order, physiological order, physical order and so on are all *samaṣṭi*.

Īśvara as physiological order

There is a physiological order. My physical body is alive and it has parts like kidneys, liver and so on. These organs function, which means they are subject to malfunction, like your car. Anything put together tends to fall apart because it is put together. I try to understand the function and malfunction in the physiological order. When students join medical college, what is it that they do? They cut a frog to try and understand the things that constitute a frog's body. From that they extrapolate to understand certain things about a human body. When they find a problem, like a malfunction of a gland, they prepare a medication. They first test the medicine on a rat. If it works, they become confident it will work on a human being. Then they try it on a monkey. If it works on a monkey, they will give it to a human being. It is science, and a discipline because of a common physiological order. It is total, *samaṣṭi*, and it is Īśvara. The physiological discipline is nothing but one physiological order.

Īśvara as psychological order

The psychological order implies the unconscious. Without the unconscious there is no psychology at all. Your responses would be purely cognitive. All I need is to make you understand, it would be sufficient. But the unconscious is strongly, often painfully, present. Many a time your response is not due to lack of understanding, it is in spite of all the understanding that you have. Despite your wisdom, culture, upbringing, you behave irrationally, because you are helpless. This is psychological order. Here, a cognitive change is important. Recognising, processing the unconscious is very important. Many good relationships are lost and many marriages break down because of the unprocessed unconscious. The spouse projects the mother or father upon the partner. It stems from the unconscious. As a child what you could not tell your parents because of the rules at home, are pushesd deep into the unconscious. Later, when you are able to trust another, like in a marriage, then the unconscious wells up. Love and trust are most conducive for the unconscious to surface. The anger you had against your mother or father is projected on to the partner. The partner does the same to you. There is so much pain and the whole relationship falls apart. It is very unfortunate that people do not recognise this fact. If they do, both can help each other to grow spiritually, even saintly.

You become a saint only when you process your unconscious. A person who has not processed his or her unconscious can never be saintly. A saintly person is one who knows pain, who has gone through pain, who has understood and assimilated pain, and who can therefore empathise with others and respond appropriately. There is an order that connects the unconscious and the emotions, that governs the emotional response to a situation. That is why there is a subject matter called psychology.

ĪŚVARA AS COGNITIVE ORDER

There is a cognitive science to understand psychology, to know that there is psychology, the unconscious, and reasons for my behaviour in a given situation. Finally everything is cognitive. The cognitive faculty, being the same everywhere, has an epistemological order. It is an order that governs what is error and what is knowledge, what can be and what cannot be, what is logical and illogical, what is rational and irrational and so on.

The human mind operates on the same framework enabling us to communicate with each other. Language operates on the basis of cognitive order. By convention, we accept a particular object be called a rose. It forms the basis for communication. Being self-conscious person, I cannot be content to know just those things that are necessary to fulfil my simple physiological and biological urges, safety, survival and other similar needs. I need to use my intellect, my thinking process, to discriminate, to choose. It is *viveka*, the most significant faculty endowed to the human organism. It is the faculty that helps me to change cognitively. Every discipline of knowledge is entirely cognitive. It is cognition and it is an order.

Memory is a definite part of this cognitive order, which, in turn, is a part of the psychological order. Memory can be either unconscious or a subliminal, subconscious conditioning. We recognise an object as a rose, because we have a memory of what a rose is. Memory is an extraordinary faculty, a very powerful floppy with an amazing capacity to store as well as to self-destruct. For instance, if I ask you details of last night's dinner, you can recall them. However, if I ask you details of a dinner six months ago, you cannot remember. You may not remember even the day of the week, let alone the details of the dinner. From this you can understand that the memory stores such details only for a few days or months and then destroys them; you cannot access them consciously. It is a wonderful programme. If it were not, your memory would be filled with trivial, insignificant details. There would be no capacity for further knowledge.

The capacity to forget is not conscious. You cannot choose to forget; it just happens. Unlike a computer programme, you cannot erase your memory. In fact, the more you try to erase memory, the stronger it becomes. It reminds me of the story of the proverbial monkey.

A teacher had promised to give a *mantra* to his disciple. Subsequently, he found that his disciple did not deserve the *mantra*. He regretted his promise and thought of a way to defuse the power of the *mantra*, without breaking his promise. He told his disciple, "I will give you the *mantra*. But when you chant the *mantra*, make sure you do not think of a monkey." Sure enough, the very next day, when the disciple began the *mantra*, his first thought was of the monkey, because he had told himself, "I must not think of a monkey." The monkey had become embedded in his memory. He would never be able to forget the monkey, not as long as he wished to chant the *mantra*. Everyone has his or her own monkey. You have your monkey which you do not wish to remember or recall. No matter how hard you try, it lingers, persists in your memory.

There is no conscious forgetting. The memory software has an inbuilt programme to destroy things that are not necessary and keeps the floppy empty for better things. By better things, it did not envisage our recalling each hurt and pain experienced. Unfortunately, these are exactly what we remember, every detail including body language and facial expressions. Our memory, our capacity to recall, to remember, is called *citta*. It is an order, and it is Īśvara.

Here, I want you to make a quantum jump. Do you know what a quantum jump is? The electron keeps jumping and every time it jumps, a photon, the particle of light, comes out. How it is going to jump, where, into which orbit, we do not know. This is the quantum jump. At the same time and place, it jumps without crossing the rules of time, space and speed. Now it is here, now there; it beats all our physical rules and we call it a quantum leap. We need to make that quantum leap here. This cognitive change is necessary.

Īśvara as dharmic order

I am a self-conscious person with a freedom to choose. My interaction with you, with the world is not completely programmed. My freewill, my choice has to be involved in any response. This element of freedom comes from the self, about which there needs to be a cognitive change. It is the freedom of the self that gives me freedom to choose at the mental level. This freedom is called freewill. The choice can be either right or wrong. Freedom to choose also implies abuse; otherwise it is not freedom. Self-consciousness and the freedom born of it, includes the possibility to abuse. So it is essential for a human being to know cognitively, very early in life, what is appropriate and what is not, in any given situation.

The propriety in my responses is already determined by the order that is Īśvara, since everything manifest is Īśvara. The possibility of a human life itself is part of the order, and we have seen that whatever is potential is manifested. The human being has the freedom to choose; it is Īśvara's software. Īśvara's knowledge has to manifest in that self-conscious being. It has to manifest in the very place, in the *buddhi*, which confers this self-consciousness and freedom.

However, there should be wisdom to understand the presence of Īśvara in my *buddhi*. Since everything is Īśvara, my *buddhi* is no exception. I see Īśvara's presence in my *buddhi*, in the form of my knowledge of right and wrong. It is what people call as conscience, inner voice. The sense of right and wrong is commonly sensed. It is a collective sense and hence universal. The sense of right and wrong is not given by Īśvara; it is Īśvara. A cognitive change is important here.

The religious people tell, you should follow your conscience; you should or should not do a particular action. They also tell you that if you go against their rules, you will suffer either in this life or in a future life. By exercising the freedom of choice and choosing rightly, you are not obliging Īśvara. There is no question of God ordering you to do this, and if you do not, he will punish you. Such concepts create fear. You have enough fear already; you do not need to convert God into yet another source of fear. If God is a source of fear, he becomes fallible. Anyone who causes fear cannot be infallible, which is why a cognitive change about God is so important for humanity. Whether you are a Christian, a Muslim, a Parsee, or a Hindu, you need to change your thinking in this area.

The inner voice, the voice of God as some people call it, is the universal sense of right and wrong. I know I should not get hurt. I do not need education to know that I should not get hurt. Every living organism, mosquitoes, bacteria and viruses, knows that it has to survive; it should not get hurt. If we take the HIV virus, it is very intelligent, although lethal to human beings. It attacks the immune system by infecting the T-cells, which are the intelligence people in our body. The immune system is thus neutralised and the infected person dies.

The desire to live is so strong that viruses and bacteria even mutate to survive. This is the nature of life. It is order and the order is Īśvara. It is clear that nobody wants to be hurt, cheated, caused pain, and so on. On the contrary, everybody wants people around to be kind, giving, compassionate, sympathetic, an endless list of positive qualities. Even a serial killer sends a mercy petition to the president of the country before his execution, hoping that he will be granted pardon. Although he did not show mercy to his victims, he expects mercy from the president. It is human nature to expect kindness without giving it in return. It is also where the problem starts. Everyone knows exactly what is right and wrong and this knowledge is universal. The universal right and wrong is what we call *dharma* and *adharma*. We commonly sense it. It is not tangible, but we sense it, like the force of gravity.

We sense it because it exists. It is *samaṣṭi* and it is Īśvara. It is not anybody's creation of right and wrong; there is no subjectivity here.

Conforming to dharma you are in harmony

Dharma is common to all, whether the person is a wealthy tycoon or an aborigine. There are different cultural forms, such as dress, hairstyles and a variety of things accepted at a given time and place; here again *dharma* is involved. By *dharma* I mean conformity to etiquette, so as not to disturb others, physically or emotionally. People tend to get disturbed and therefore you try not to disturb. Conformity is not a commonplace response; it is not a response of the weak. Conformity is the response of the wise who do not want to disturb others and who do not think they lose by conforming. Their response is born of awareness, of clear thinking, and that is important. You conform, not out of fear, but because of understanding. You need not conform totally, you can set your own trend, but with some editing. Whatever you do can be in keeping with what is prevalent, nothing drastic. Conformity born of understanding is beauty; like a symphony, where there are hundreds of instruments making beautiful music. If one person decides to change the pitch of his instrument, because he wants to be heard, he will never be heard afterwards. There is beauty in conformity, but it has to come from wisdom, courage, and understanding.

There is something unique in each society at a given time and place, and there again, conformity has a value.

The value is to be a person of least resistance; your presence gels with the whole situation. You do not become incongruous in the whole set up. It is not an ordinary thing. It is what Īśvara is; what *dharma* is, what harmony is. Lord Kṛṣṇa repeatedly talks of harmony in the *Gītā*. He says, "Set your mind with mine and perform an action. Surrender everything to me and do what is to be done." What does he mean when he asks you to surrender? Where do you find Kṛṣṇa asking you to surrender? It is not said, but it is to be understood. It means to fall in line with *dharma*, the order, is to surrender to Īśvara.

One side of the order is *dharma*, the other is *karma*. If you go against *dharma*, the law, then it rubs you. To rub against the law is to get rubbed in the process; that is law. For instance, rub against an old gnarled tree, a tamarind tree, with your bareback. Scrub yourself against the tree. A few minutes later, turn and look at the tree. Nothing has happened to the trunk; perhaps an old piece of bark or two has dropped off, which is good for the tree. Now, feel your back, the soreness and the pain; you will not be able to wear any clothes for days until it heals. This is *dharma*, if you rub against it. Nothing happens to the order of *dharma*, but everything happens to you.

Dharma and *karma* are two sides of the order. Īśvara is both *dharma* and *karma*. He is manifest as the law of *dharma* and *karma*. You cannot get away with rubbing against the law. If you do rub against the law, it is of your own freewill, it has its consequences. Any action born of freewill will produce a result, be it prayer, a helping hand, reaching out to others. All are within the law of *dharma* and there is total freedom to perform these actions. They definitely yield results.

It is empathy that makes you reach out to help others. Īśvara is present in the form of empathy in the human heart. A human being without empathy does not exist. It is your natural response to others' pain. I cannot give a better example than that of a tennis player who has won the Wimbledon title in a five-setter match. He is ecstatic. He throws his racket in the air and kisses the ground. He then walks up to the net to shake the opponent's hand which is the convention. The opponent is disappointed, his face crest fallen. If you watch the face of the man who has won, who was ecstatic just a minute ago, you will see a change in his expression. The joy is replaced by sadness. It is empathy. He cannot be ecstatic when he shakes hands with the man across the net. He knows what it is like to lose; he has been on that side often enough. His face reflects the other man's disappointment. The human heart is imbued with this great capacity to empathise. It is empathy which makes us share, reach out, give and so on. It is an expression of Īśvara. We can say say that Īśvara has given himself, through the human form, the capacity to empathise.

It is not totally wrong if you do not reach out to the person in pain. Yet when you do reach out and help, you are doing what is expected of you, rather, what you would expect in a similar situation. In reaching out, there is a sense of satisfaction. You feel good because you are in touch with *dharma* that is Īśvara.

Adharma is also Īśvara. If that is so, why do you not feel good when you do *adharma*? You commit *adharma* because of inner pressure from your likes and dislikes, *rāga* and *dveṣa*. You can be pressurised only if your ego is very much present there, which means there is more of you and less of Īśvara. Every time you cut corners, when you compromise with your value system, you are under emotional pressure. It makes you compromise values you are well aware of. The resultant hurt, guilt and regret makes you suffer. Yielding to your inner pressure is a very unfortunate situation.

When you conform to *dharma*, there is a visible satisfaction since there is no pressure. The person whom you helped may or may not express his or her thanks but you are happy that you were able to help. The joy is palpable and we call it *dṛṣṭa-phala*, seen result. Beyond this visible result, your helpful action creates an invisible, unseen result called *adṛṣṭa-phala*. This *adṛṣṭa-phala* is called *puṇya*. Though *puṇya* is a matter of belief, it has some logic behind it. *Śāstra* talks about *puṇya, adṛṣṭa-phala,* which you can assimilate because it stands to reason.

When a person is at the right place at the right time, you require a word to explain that person's situation, because it is human experience. In English it is called luck, and every language has an equivalent word for luck. Sometimes things go your way and everything clicks, while there are times when nothing seems to be right. There appears to be some hidden, but tangible force behind these experiences. Astrology tries to find the time period when circumstances can work for you and when they will not. It is not the planets that cast their influence. Astrology is merely a predicting discipline. It is a particular model and it works. In fact, it is all Īśvara, including the law of *karma*. It is this law of *karma*, its influence that is explained in the form of Jupiter, Saturn, Mercury, Venus and so on. When you propitiate Saturn, it is Īśvara that you propitiate. Therefore, here again a cognitive change is necessary, for there are such things as positive and negative forces, *puṇya* and *pāpa*.

When you take advantage of a situation, you are going against *dharma* and it is definitely *pāpa-karma*. It is an action and it attracts result which may fructify now or later. *Puṇya* and *pāpa* are responsible for pleasant and unpleasant experiences in life.

Somebody asked me, 'If everything is Īśvara, why is there suffering?' Suffering or enjoyment is due to your *karma* alone. It is because Īśvara being everything is not clearly understood. That cognitive change has not taken place. If it has, then there will be suffering, certainly, but there will not be emotional pain. You will have physical or situational pain, but you will be objective. If you are together as a person, you can face unpleasant situations objectively; if not you become as unpleasant as the situation is. You will require help from another to deal with the problem. You also become a problem for the person who helps you making the situation more complicated.

Situations are not constant; they are variable, either pleasant or unpleasant. If you are objective, you do not yield to the pressures of right and wrong. You use your freewill wisely. Unfortunately, your freewill is also under pressure. When your *rāga-dveṣa,* likes and dislikes pressurise you, the freewill is the first casualty. It is a hostage in the hands of likes and dislikes. Despite your intelligence and wisdom, your will is weakened and the *rāga-dveṣa* complete their work. Your likes and dislikes may not rob you of your wisdom, but they can and do rob your will. This is the time for you to seek help by invoking the grace of Īśvara.

Talk 7

Invoking Īśvara

Human life has to be lived intelligently. I have always wondered what is intelligent living. I have a number of possibilities, but finally I settled for one. To seek help when you need is intelligent living. If you have a headache, you reach for an aspirin. If the pain persists, you consult a doctor. This is intelligent living. When you need help, you should be able to recognise that you need help. Sometimes, the help is not at hand, then you seek help elsewhere. Seeking help elsewhere is exactly where Īśvara comes, in the form of prayer. You invoke his grace. Grace is nothing but *karma-phala,* which is a potential. Īśvara is manifest not merely on the surface. There is much that is not visible and depends entirely on your effort to manifest. Your effort includes using your freewill, based on your wisdom. Yoiur wisdom throws up the options in any given situation and you use my freewill to choose and act.

Need for prayer

Over and above your efforts, your enthusiasm, enterprise, wisdom, knowledge, infrastructure, assets, there is one more factor, which makes the difference between success and failure. This factor is your past *karma,* which you can neutralise by prayer alone because it is *adṛṣṭa,* unseen. If you have to handle an unseen force, you can do so only with another unseen force. *Adṛṣṭa* is a potential and before it fructifies, you create another force to counter it. This is the basis of prayer.

Prayer is totally deliberate

Prayer is the only action that enjoys the total freedom coming from your freewill. It is the only action where your will is completely free. In a distressing situation, you can cry, scream, rage, reach out for pills; you can do anything except pray because prayer has to come from me, from your deliberate freewill. When you choose to pray, you create a force out of your action which helps you handle situations where no other help is available.

Prayer involves understanding the total

Prayer helps you recognise that as an individual, there is the total. It also helps you recognise the difference between the two. In this recognition, Īśvara, the whole, pervades you, the individual, just as the ocean pervades the wave. The wave can appreciate the ocean as the almighty, even though it does not fully understand what it takes to be almighty. The wave can invoke the ocean as the Lord, as an altar. Invoking the ocean as an altar, the wave can obtain a result born of prayer. The difference between the individual and the total continues.

Īśvara pervades you; not just you, he pervades this entire *jagat*. The entire *jagat* is a manifestation of Īśvara, with all the potentials, the possibilities. You can choose and tap any potential which is why you have different types of *karma*.

In prayer, you have physical rituals, fire rituals and so on. You have oral prayer. You also have mental prayer, that is meditation. You need to understand that meditation is also prayer.

What is meditation?

I feel that a cognitive change is needed here because people think meditation is something different. They think it involves breathing in a particular way or sitting in particular postures, or watching a particular spot like the tip of your nose or between the brows. Meditation is defined as *saguṇa-brahma-viṣaya-mānasa-vyāpāraḥ,* mental activity with Brahman, Īśvara as the object. In meditation, only the mind is involved, hence it is *mānasa-vyāpāra.* You can create an altar for yourself mentally and pray. It is meditation. It is not posture or breathing or looking at something.

Nobody worships an idol

Idol worship is another area where you need cognitive change. Some people ask me the reason for worshipping idols. 'Why do Hindus worship idols?' Nobody worships idols. You worship only the Lord when you invoke the Lord in a particular form. When every form is the Lord, any form is good enough to invoke the total. If someone wants to draw your attention, he can touch your arm or even your little finger. You respond as a complete individual. But if your little finger is hurt, your entire attention is on that finger. The doctor who treats it also tends to that finger. Finally, the bill is not given to the little finger, but to you, the whole of you.

YOU CAN INVOKE ĪŚVARA IN ANY FORM

If every form, including the formless space, is Īśvara's manifestation, the material cause that has manifested as the *jagat* becomes the altar to invoke the maker. The form is the altar for the maker. So the description of Rāma or Kṛṣṇa becomes the form and altar to invoke the Lord. It makes no difference. You can invoke Īśvara in any particular form. The maker is invoked in the material, in a manifest form, just as you are available in this physical form to transact with the world. If you want to congratulate a scientist for his or her brilliant discovery, you shake the person's hand. Your congratulation has nothing to do with the shaken hands. It is the conscious being that is admired and congratulated. Your respect is for him, the whole person. Similarly, you invoke Īśvara in a given form. The form is a symbol of the whole, but it is not the form that you worship. You worship only Īśvara.

Human life is lived in terms of forms and forms alone. Life is manifest in forms. Language is form, script is form, everything is form. People decided by convention to give form to letters such as *a*, *e*, *u* and so on, which is why you have so many different scripts. It is all form. Thank God that you have forms coming down to you, because to create a form and connect it to the Lord is not an ordinary thing. You know how difficult it is to create brand awareness in the market place. For example, to connect soap with Lux in people's minds, the company has spent millions of rupees, over the years. Yet their share of the market is limited. Lot of effort, planning, strategy, and money are spent on advertisements, just to gain a small percentage of the market.

Over a period of time, a connection between the soap and the brand is created. That particular soap, Lux for example, becomes the person's favourite brand, his or her *iṣṭa*.

If this is the effort required to create a connection, you are very lucky to have so many forms coming down to without any effort or expenditure on your part. We must thank your forefathers and ancestors for this. Rāma, Kṛṣṇa, Jesus, Allah, are all names of Īśvara. If I ask you to think of the Lord, the form that first comes to your mind is your *iṣṭa-devatā*. There is a need for cognitive change here.

It is wonderful that you have a form to worship. Physical worship is possible only when there is an altar to place a flower. You offer the flower, and as an individual you invoke the total. The total, *samaṣṭi*, that is Īśvara, can be invoked anywhere. If you want to touch the ocean, what will you touch? Will you touch a wave or will you travel by ship and touch the entire ocean? Obviously, you will touch the nearest wave. When you touch the wave, you are touching the ocean. You can worship the ocean also, since you can invoke the Lord in any form.

The bronze statues in our country are easy targets for thieves. People ask me, "Why don't the Gods do something? Why do they allow themselves to be stolen?" They do not understand that those who steal do not look upon the bronze idols as Gods. Moreover, their *karma* will take care of their actions, either now or later. Another question I am asked often, "Swamiji, why do you allow people to do *namaskāra* to you? Are you not encouraging people to idolise you?"

I tell them, "It is part of our culture, our tradition. It is their way of showing respect and I respect their custom. That is all." They are not worshipping the person in the Swami. They respect the robes for what they signify. If anyone thinks that the respect is for the person, it will destroy the person.

You must understand that there is nothing better than a physical action to convert an emotion. Without the action, the emotion will disappear as a passing fancy. It gains strength only when you express the emotion physically. The custom of exchanging gifts is an expression of your emotions. Come Christmas, you find that everybody goes shopping. They buy gifts and pack them beautifully. A gift becomes an object of your greeting, your friendship, an expression of your love, and your wishes. These are physically expressed. Even a flimsy emotion becomes a reality by this rich *kāyika-karma,* physical action. It is the greatest thing our culture has to offer to the world, to humanity. You express the wishes in your heart through physical actions.

In a lighter vein, there is another angle to this. You can give a gift and also forget about it. This person went into a shop to buy some cards. He looked into all the shelves but could not find the right card with the right lines. The shop assistant asked him if he needed help. He said, "Oh, I want a special card for the one I love." The shop assistant gave him a wide selection of cards. The man found just what he was looking for and was delighted. "Please give me a dozen of these cards." The shop assistant was curious. He looked into the card, and much to his amusement, it read,

"You are the only one I love." It is possible to send cards without deep feelings, that is, to have forms without content.

The rich tradition of culture and worship that you have inherited, have so much to give to the world. Many others have lost their forms, their altar, and their traditions because of religious aggression. They have lost their culture, and even their language. This aggression continues to destroy other cultures, even now. They have not understood the importance of forms in worship. They need to change cognitively. You can see clearly it is not the form that you worship. You invoke the Lord in the form and worship that Lord with flowers and rituals. It is something very beautiful. It is a blessing. You can invoke Īśvara as the sun or you can invoke him in the sun. There is a difference. Just as in medicine, there are broad-spectrum drugs and specific drugs, you have broad-spectrum prayers and specific prayers. Propitiating Saturn or the Sun is a specific prayer. Bhagavān will understand; there is no confusion. If someone is critical of this form of worship, it is because they do not understand it. As you pray you find the prayer transforms you. It is not easy to do *namaskāra* to an altar. The ego is too big to allow that. If others are able to do so, what prevents you? Your reluctance could well be some anger against your father which is why some people worship only mother Goddess. Either way it is acceptable, you can worship God as father or mother or both.

Prayer, as I said earlier, can be physical, oral or mental. A prayer that is *mānasa-karma,* mental action, is meditation. There are certain groups who invent sounds for meditation.

They claim that the sound, *mantra*, is specifically chosen for each person. Chanting a meaningless sound is certainly not meditation. A *mantra* is not meaningless. Every *mantra* has a meaning.

Intelligent living is to seek help through prayer

Prayer is a means to seek help from Īśvara. Seeking the help of Īśvara is intelligent living, because you seek help from an infallible source. Somebody wanted to know the meaning of infallible. Infallible is that which cannot fail, which cannot commit mistakes. Everything here is Īśvara, the laws, the order; Īśvara is both the maker and the material cause. If all that is here is one order, then the Lord is infallible because of the order. Therefore, Īśvara is the only infallible source. You have the capacity to will and invoke the Lord. If your will is under the spell of *rāga* and *dveṣa*, Rāvaṇa and Kumbhakarṇa, all you can do is pray, 'O Lord, please help me.' This is intelligent living. To seek help when it is needed is intelligent living.

Seeking help is not one more desire. It has to be very clearly understood. Desires are never a problem. In fact, Lord Kṛṣṇa says, "In a human being, I am in the form of desire that is not against *dharma*.[8]" You can have any number of desires as long as they are within *dharma*. There is no problem with having desires. Another person said, "Swamiji, I have too many ambitions." Ambition is also desire. Then, where does ambition end and greed begin?

---

8 *dharmāviruddho bhūteṣu kāmo'smi bharatarṣabha* (*Bhagavad Gītā* 7.11)

If, in the process of fulfilling your ambition, you cross the limits of *dharma*, then it is greed. In Rishikesh, there was a *sādhu*. His life's ambition was to have a stainless steel begging bowl. His heart was set on it and even if Bhagavān were to appear before him, he would ask only for a stainless steel bowl. To get a stainless steel bowl, if he steals from another *sādhu*, it becomes greed. If you want to take over another company, it is not greed if you keep within *dharma*.

The more you keep within *dharma*, the more you are in touch with Īśvara. Īśvara expresses through you. The more you appreciate Īśvara, the less of you is there. Less of you means less of your smallness, your fear, your anxiety. Fear and anxiety are born of the unconscious alone. The fear that you cannot handle fear is because when there is fear, you fear that you have fear; like a chain it goes on and on. When there is fear, say aloud, "I welcome fear. It is another manifestation of Īśvaras. I welcome it. I am not afraid of fear." It is part of the psychological order and it is Īśvara. If you understand this, then Īśvara will guide your life. In this understanding, some cognitive change has taken place about you, the self. Here again, you are not what you think you are. When you are happy, you do not think about yourself and that is what you are. It is an insight you need to have. The knowledge has to grow upon you. That is what Vedanta teaches.

So far, I have been talking of *yoga*. It is your self-growth, insight and clarity. More than that, only Vedanta can give you. I do not believe that anyone can be happy in today's world without Vedanta. It is not possible because our society is born of competition, nurtured in competition. The competition starts from the cradle. It is a society of competition. Naturally, our lot is very complex.

We need Vedanta to be sane and we have to solve the problem fundamentally. There is no partial solution. Relative happiness is not possible for us. When we cannot be relatively happy, the best thing is, go for the whole. Go for the absolute solution. It is the only way; there is no other way. The humanity has placed itself in a corner, driven itself into a corner from where it has no other solution except to know, "I am the whole." It is what Vedanta is.

Oṁ tat sat

Books by Swami Dayananda Saraswati

Public Talk Series :

1. Living Intelligently
2. Need for Cognitive Change
3. Discovering Love
4. Successful Living
5. The Value of Values
6. Vedic View and Way of Life

Upaniṣad Series :

7. Muṇḍakopaniṣad
8. Kenopaniṣad

Moments with Oneself Series :

9. Freedom from Helplessness
10. Living versus Getting On
11. Insights
12. Action and Reaction
13. The Fundamental Problem
14. Problem is You, Solution is You
15. Purpose of Prayer
16. Vedanta 24x7
17. Freedom
18. Crisis Management
19. Surrender and Freedom
20. The Need for Personal Reorganisation
21. Freedom in Relationship
22. Stress-free Living

Text Translation Series :

23. Śrīmad Bhagavad Gītā
    (Text with roman transliteration and English translation)

Stotra Series :

24. Dipārādhanā
25. Prayer Guide
    (With explanations of several Mantras, Stotras, Kirtans and Religious Festivals)

Bhagavad Gītā Series :

26. Bhagavad Gītā Home Study Program
    Vol 1-4 (Hardbound)
27. Bhagavad Gītā Home Study Program
    Vol 1-4 (Softbound)

Meditation Series :

28. Morning Meditation-prayers

Essays :

29. Do all Religions have the same goal?
30. Conversion is Violence
31. Gurupūrṇimā
32. Dānam
33. Japa
34. Can We?
35. **Teaching Tradition of Advaita Vedanta**

Exploring Vedanta Series : (*vākyavicāra*)

36. śraddhā bhakti dhyāna yogād avaihi
    ātmānaṁ ced vijānīyāt

Books by Smt. Sheela Balaji

37. Salutations to Rudra
    (based on the exposition of Śrī Rudram by Swami Dayananda Saraswati)
38. Without a Second

Also available at :

ARSHA VIDYA RESEARCH
AND PUBLICATION TRUST
32/4 Sir Desika Road
Mylapore Chennai 600 004
Telefax : 044 - 2499 7131
Email : avrandpc@gmail.com

ARSHA VIDYA GURUKULAM
Anaikatti P.O.
Coimbatore 641 108
Ph : 0422 - 2657001
Fax : 0422 - 2657002
Email : office@arshavidya.in

ARSHA VIDYA GURUKULAM
P.O.Box 1059. Pennsylvania
PA 18353, USA.
Ph : 001-570-992-2339
Email : avp@epix.net

SWAMI DAYANANDA ASHRAM
Purani Jhadi, P.B. No. 30
Rishikesh, Uttaranchal 249 201
Telefax : 0135-2430769
Email : ashrambookstore@yahoo.com

AND IN ALL THE LEADING BOOK STORES, INDIA